Twin Mum Truths

Hayley Zemontas

BookLeaf Publishing

Twin Mum Truths © 2023 Hayley Zemontas

All rights reserved.

No part of this publication may be reproduced, stored in a retrieval system, or transmitted, in any form or by any means, electronic, mechanical, photocopying, recording or otherwise, without the prior written permission of the presenters.

Hayley Zemontas asserts the moral right to be identified as author of this work.

Presentation by *BookLeaf Publishing*

Web: www.bookleafpub.com

E-mail: info@bookleafpub.com

ISBN: 9789357441285

First edition 2023

For my 2 favourite humans in the whole world, the ones who've made me a Mother. Daisy and Lea, thank you for enriching my life and teaching me so much about the world, my capabilities and love without conditions. I love you infinitely.

You Got This

For all the other twin Mamas out there,
days after birth or starting to prepare,
my message is, YOU GOT THIS.
You'll have days where you feel like giving up,
like you're drained dry with nothing left in your
cup.
You'll curse all the parents who gave birth to a
single baby,
rant and moan that they've had it so easy.
Some days, it can seem an impossible task
to juggle two infants, put your needs last.
But whether you're a single parent or in a
partnership,
take any offer of help, every little bit.
Because you have two newborns; it's hard and
you're allowed to admit it.
Just know that YOU GOT THIS.

For all the Mamas waiting patiently for their
time,
each month with bated breath, hoping for blue
lines,
I say with conviction, YOU GOT THIS.
It's awful having to put on a front,

congratulating those who have everything you
want.
Maybe you're searching for a soulmate
or you've taken the route,
of going it alone and raising your brood.
Whether you're trying for children without
success,
or enduring fertility treatments and tests,
you're a warrior, nothing less.
Stay hopeful, YOU GOT THIS.

For all the pregnant Mamas struggling to get by,
with fluid-filled ankles and stretch marked
thighs,
I promise YOU GOT THIS.
It's fine if you don't enjoy every minute;
you can be thankful for the blessing, yet still
wish it were finished.
Whether you've suffered with sickness or found
it a breeze,
relished every flutter and pee'd when you
sneezed,
trust me, it's all gonna be worth it.
Honestly, YOU GOT THIS.

For all the Mamas just trying their best,
giving their all with very little rest,
YOU GOT THIS.
Some days suck but you still show up.

You cherish the smooth and ride out the rough,
and dole out every last piece of love.
You'll have days idyllic and others fraught,
but Mama you can survive it all,
because of these little humans you've made.
They bring light, laughter and irreversible
change,
and a fiery love that never fades.
They're yours; YOU GOT THIS.

Empty

All of us here are empty.
A roomful of clams, awaiting our pearls;
nervous spines, like question marks curled.
Anticipation, tasting metallic on our tongue.
A flash of fire in our eyes; warriors strong.

We pack our hearts within ribbed shells,
trying to protect against the pitiful swell.
A wave of hope, of hopelessness;
still resolute, we ride that crest.

We're focused on that joyous light,
a natural event for which we fight,
and fight.
Fight some more.
Counting, clinging to numbers galore.

Magic drugs on days 2 till 6.
Wearing bruises bright from crook to wrists.
Trembling hands around plastic cups,
sipping constant coffee with twisted guts.

The doctors are kind, the tests intrusive.
We sacrifice all that we can give.
Endure the treatments, lay ourselves bare

Just women desperate, hungry and scared.

A head full of fears wrestling with quiet faith.
There's a battle in progress, it's whatever it takes.
Hear the cries of the brave lioness;
the roar of the blessed and sadly bereft.

It's a song which echoes within each soul,
a call to war from a deep, black hole.
An aching abyss we've tried to fill,
yet watched our dreams seep and spill.

Yet still, we've rallied, pushed forth and fought,
aching for the moon so taut.
Waiting for that moment when we're empty no
more.

We'll Tell Our Children

This isn't how it was meant to be.
No proud pregnant bumps beaconing the streets.
This isn't how we envisioned growing, holding
new life,
Mum's everywhere, bent double with the weight
of blossoming bones and uncertainty, rife.
A hidden threat; we're running terrified.
Paralysed.
Anxiety marring the gloss of celebration,
a time of joy dripping in devastation.

All the time worrying for our family,
both those on the outside, and the new one
slowly budding within.
We're so desperate to guard the treasures beneath
our skin;
we'll fight like lionesses, as Mothers we'll do
anything.
We've carried them this far, not without trials.
Faced sickness, cramps, the sting of needles
stealing our blood in vials.
A pandemic can't help but crumple our smiles,
at a time when we're already a vulnerable soup
of hormones that surge, crest and stoop.
We're frightened, panicked, confused;

so many questions, worries and blues.
No place for reassurance because no one has a
clue!
Just a constant siren in our heads screaming
'what should I do?'.

How do we protect these tiny beings whom we
love?
Are we doing what's right, are we good enough?
Will I, can I ever be strong enough
to navigate the smooth and inevitably rough?

Of course, we will always find a way.
We've made it here to this very day,
and that's pretty good.
We'll tell our children we DID and we COULD,
even when we thought we never would.
At the eye of the storm, we pulled together
showing kindness, hope and weaving stories to
keep forever.

Tales, memories part of a National history.
Our children, they'll learn about this at school
one day,
study the text books and be able to say
'My Mummy carried me throughout this fray'.
No, this isn't how it was supposed to be;
we didn't expect to be pregnant during Covid 19.
Our normal life suspended, routine upended;

a tragedy nobody could have foreseen.
Bringing life into a world overrun with death;
we're all scared parents just trying our best.

Now, as well as fretting about labour and scans,
all our shopping trips, catch ups and best laid
plans,
have been scattered to the wind in a fistful of
sand.
We're having to rethink, regroup, readjust;
place trust in our government and our own
dogged strength.

But from tragedy, came the true colours of the
human spirit,
hope tentative and trembling yet, nothing could
kill it.
Streaked bright as the rainbows tacked across
window panes,
we'll tell our children of the glorious shades.
How the world did falter, then shone dazzling
once again.
We'll tell them we lived through Covid 19,
and woke to an existence
more beautiful,
more appreciable,
than we had ever before seen.

Carrying Two

Amongst a crowd of burgeoning Mothers,
in a strangers glazed stare, I saw my own.
An expression I'd worn just 6 months ago.
I recognised the shimmer of incredulous tears,
racing thoughts that flicked through the
oncoming years.
Imaginary photos without the camera flash,
spilling past her eyes, as her world spun on its
axis,
gave a dull crash.
I knew how it felt to seem suspended, reality
suddenly upended.
Feeling both heavy with shock, yet feather light;
coasting on the wings of a miracle, torn between
fear and utter delight.
There's time enough for worries, for now just
soak it up;
a moment so many long for, it's yours to keep, to
touch.
To relive, retell and stick in the memory book so
that you might recall even 10 years down the
line,
this spark of colour, frozen in time,
like a pendant of amber encasing a fly.
Bask in the news; you're chosen, you're strong.

Strong enough to carry two instead of one.
You're a vessel of the most wondrous kind,
a parcel with the most precious cargo inside.
It's natural to feel trepidation and doubt,
to struggle to breathe as you process this clout.
But someday soon, you'll laugh and shout
because you're a twin mama and hugely proud.
Be proud, be loud, bask in the glory-
this is the first page of the rest of your story.
A whole new chapter on silken parchment,
embossed in gold;
a recollection that can never grow old.
The day the world faltered not once, but twice,
and handed you a gift for which there's no price.

My Girls

My girls.

Signalled by cramps and 2 blue lines.
I carried you from grains of rice,
hardly dared to believe that you would survive,
that something this golden could ever be mine.
But sure enough, however rough,
at 8 weeks I took a glimpse inside.
And there you were, perfect works of art.
Nestled safe next to my heart,
just the size of 2 budding grapes;
a whole world, slowly taking shape.

My girls.

New life daubed on a canvas torn.
I carried you throughout a storm;
battled fear, an uncertain swarm.
I kept you swaddled beneath skin so warm.
I laughed, I cried but could always find
a smile for your wriggling, innocent forms.
You blossomed from mangoes to papayas long;
your lullaby, my heart beats song.
Amongst chaos, your legs uncurled
to show at last, my precious girls.

So Full

Once your babies are born,
you're gonna feel so full.
Full of wonder, full of love,
full of the feeling that you can never get enough
of gazing upon your newborn's face.
That first moment, time can never erase.
You're gloriously, joyously full.
But as you shower and slough off the day,
wash the grime and fatigue of birth away,
you'll suddenly realise now, who you are,
face to face with a raw caesarean scar.
And rawer still, your stomach once round,
taut and shining; an orb profound,
now is tender, boggy and strange.
And as euphoria starts to fade,
you might feel empty, and that's okay.

Once your babies are born,
you'll feel a little empty.
Flat and aching, a soulless nest;
both hollow and heavy within your chest.
In this moment, you're vulnerable and sore,
exhaustion seeps from every pore
and, your womb is so suddenly bare.
But, as you mourn the loss of your pregnant self,

a completely new person is birthed as well.
As you watch those perfect hands unfurl,
to wrap tight around your finger curled,
your eyes will seep and your heart will sing
as you try on this unfamiliar skin.
You're a Mother now, both soft and strong;
the piece that's been missing all along.
Some days, the emptiness will hit you still,
but ultimately, you'll feel so fulfilled.

Another Planet Entirely

It'll change your life.
That's what they say.
But you can't truly comprehend it, until that day
and all the infinite days to come.
All at once they're your world, your moon and
sun.
You're gonna find colours you never knew
existed.
The way they nestle to your body is the piece
that you never knew you'd been missing.
There'll be moments when you miss the 'before'.
A yearning for sleep, so hard to ignore.
There'll be nights when you barely feel the
sheets at all;
uninterrupted kip, now a distant memory.
Once a realm of bliss, the nights become your
enemy.
You'll swap languishing baths for quick fire
showers,
arms aching as they rock that wailing bundle for
hours.
But then you'll gaze upon that face innocent as a
flower,
still so raw, so beautifully new,
and it'll settle a little easier,

fit a little neater, this other version of you.

It'll change your life.
That's what they say.
And it's true in every single way.
Priorities take a drastic shift,
your needs and wants now bottom of the list.
At first there'll be chaos, no kind of routine.
Just shuffling from task to task on repeat;
constant responding to every need,
every whimper, wail and scream.
And you'll wonder what it felt like to experience
peace.
Those tiny snatched moments, you'll appreciate
so much more,
but don't wish the time away because it truly
does soar,
and suddenly your babies aren't so small.

It'll change your life.
That's what they say.
Give you reserves of strength to conquer and
slay,
as something primal comes awake.
You'll become attuned to their every cry,
find it hard to remember such a time
when you didn't dissolve in the blue of their
eyes.

Sure, there'll be days when you've just had
enough,
when your resolve is chipped and the ground too
rough.
You're lost and stranded without a map,
just muddling through, trying to stay on track.
Be prepared, your life will irrevocably change.
You've entered a kingdom baffling and strange,
with mountains and conquests at every stage.
Motherhood, a land where love blooms fiery.
You're now part of another planet entirely.

Newborn Nights

Now, I'm part of the night.
A stitch in it's fabric, a star in the sky.
Cradling my offspring tight.
Rather than missing my empty bed,
wishing for a pillow beneath my head,
I'm savouring these moments instead.
I'm looking at you, drinking you in,
choosing the life of a Mother with twins.
Feeling alive, at one with the world
even when, I'm so tired it hurts.
The lack of rest pales compared to the worth,
the value of these precious shared hours.
For, I know babyhood is quickly devoured.
Already, a whole month has passed;
proof that a lifetime can zoom in a flash.
You're filling out, losing that newborn sheen,
becoming tiny people of whom I've dreamed.
And I'm becoming someone else too,
still me but with pieces entirely new.
I'm still settling within this new skin,
adjusting to a huge responsibility.
Adoration, a bond I'd always hoped to feel.
Connections slowly forged and sealed.
I would spend long, sleepless nights caressing
the shapes of your movements inside,

as I stretched and grew to the size of the moon,
our heartbeats enmeshed within a cocoon.
Now, I'm still awake at 3AM
staring in wonder at my babies again;
my body still a crib to keep you safe.
But these days, I'm studying every inch of your
face,
features in miniature; such perfection I've made.
The caterpillar curl of a hand wrapped around
one of my fingers, forever bound.
Like climbing roses, we are entwined
by blood, by love and everlasting light.
I love you for all the days, and these crazy
newborn nights.

Double The Love

I'm a Mum.
A Mum of twins.
That's two car seats, two high chairs,
two infants to lug up and down the stairs.
That's no hands left for anything else;
double commitments,
not much time for myself.
It's learning how to balance and juggle,
heavy arms giving constant cuddles.
It's brain fog, cups of tea gone cold;
endless piles of washing to fold.
It's sleep deprivation, barely able to function;
I've changed my mind thanks, I'll get off at the
junction!
It's feeling I can't carry on anymore,
then the triumph in just getting out of the door.
It's fear when I realised, this is forever.
But they smiled at me, and we're in this together.
It's twice the hormones- that's a lot of tears!
A heavy rucksack filled with guilt and fears.
Do they receive equal love and time?
And such trauma when leaving one to cry,
because I cannot split myself in two.
But, despite all that I push on through.
Twins are double trouble, that's what others say,

and it's true, it's hard work everyday.
But don't forget the enormous amount of love,
that for my children I'm more than enough.
I'm their safe port through every storm,
a place of security from dusk till dawn.
What an amazing privilege it is
to watch their journey, and all its climbs and
dips.
Helping tiny people to navigate life,
to see them learn, flourish and thrive.
The responsibility can weigh a ton;
not every day is rainbows and fun.
Sometimes, it's tantrums and patience testing,
discovering boundaries and button pressing.
It's needing a break but there are no days off;
it's a 24 hour ride without any stops.
It's exhaustion juxtaposed with glee;
wondering how I ever lived without this missing
piece.
I'm unable to remember an existence when
my every moment didn't revolve around them.
That's a parents blessing as well as a curse;
the best job in the world but, some days are the
worst.
There's colic, croup and teething pains;
we just get over one thing, for it all to start
again.
There are bumps and hurdles at every stage,
but I forget them all once we've turned the page.

I find myself missing my babes in arms,
nostalgic for those magical parts.
It's watching my babies continually change;
blooming with pride but also heartache
as they become more independent each day.
It's not knowing who to turn to first,
pulled so many ways it hurts.
Adapting my approach to suit the need;
remembering they're two people, separate and
unique,
trying to make quality time for each.
Parenting twins is an arduous task
but, it gets a little easier as time does pass.
The coat of motherhood starts to fit
more comfortably, the longer I wear it.
It becomes a second, seamless skin;
settles like mist as our journey begins.
From the moment our children are mere
seedlings,
we love and protect these innocent things.
I'm lucky, I've always had double the wonder,
double the sunshine and lungs loud as thunder.
I experienced sickness magnified,
carried them till I stretched towards the sky.
Now, I can't imagine one ever feeling enough,
because I'm a Mum of twins
and that's double the love.

Me

I'm still getting used to being one again.
A singular, separate person again.
I love the word 'Mummy'- it's my favourite thing
to be.
But I'm also remembering, there are other parts
of me,
more puzzle pieces that I treasure equally.
I'd forgotten how it feels to wander down the
street,
unencumbered by pushchairs, bags, nappies,
independent of my children; lighter, free.
We all need sometimes, a little space,
but I'd be lying if I said I didn't miss your face.
Those little faces copied and pasted from mine,
uniquely perfect; minutely divine.
You've become the very core of my life,
around which the stars spin and the planets
align.
I guess all I'm trying hard to say,
is I'm torn between both- Motherhood and work,
and I think that's okay?
Before you came along, support work was my
love,
a reason to breathe, to succeed and get up.
But it just takes a shuffle, an adjustment of sorts,

to find the right balance, set the right course.
There's way more room in my heart than I'd
thought;
you can love your children but need time apart
too.
You can feel lost without them but also
somehow, like you.
All lessons I'm learning as a parent, new.
At the end of a work day when I walk through
my door,
that bit of a break means I love you even more,
and I'm enraptured once again by your smiles
galore.
The way you hold out your arms, reaching high,
and I swing you up to kick the sky.
I breathe in your smell, pressing close;
that's what I really love the most.
Coming back to you, shedding that coat.
I'm Mummy again.
I'm me.
I'm home.

Close Enough

She's up on her feet now.
Little, mighty legs that carry her across the floor,
like a drunkard, weaving into walls and doors.
She pulls herself up seamlessly,
circuits the room easily.
She's still gaining the confidence to let go
completely.
Right now, she clings loosely to my hands
but, I know soon enough she'll break those
bands,
and she'll be off all on her own.
One day, she'll suddenly find the courage to let
go,
and I'll smile and clap as my heart breaks, slow.
Because it's both beautiful and painful to watch
you grow,
grow away from me.
And I know it's only harder from here on out,
as you start to run further and your wings will
sprout.
Right now, you're my shadow, an extension of
my arm,
a trusting hand inside my palm.
I want to keep you close enough,
to shield you from all harm.

Once, my body was the shell around yours;
to cradle you safe whilst your organs formed.
And you slept to the beat of my pulsing heart;
beneath my skin, you'd skitter and dart.
We were barely separate beings, more a
collection of parts,
tethered together by a rippling cord;
nutrients flowing from my body to yours.
As Mother's, we give our blood, our breath;
some days, every ounce of strength.
We sleep, then wake and do it all once again,
and with each passing day, the farther we must
reach,
watching as independence creeps.
Suddenly, you want to do things without me.
It rips me in half, I'm torn at the seams,
both so proud yet yearning to keep
you as a babe in my arms, close to my chest,
close enough to feel every breath.
I still sniff your head for that baby smell,
and feel relief that the scent still does dwell.
But, I know it's only a matter of time;
you're toddling now but one day you'll soar and
fly,
make your own journey into the sky.
My heart will splinter and break, as I smile and
wave,
watching you take the path you've paved.
I can't stop you from peeling away,

but I'll be there throughout the smooth and the
rough.
All I can do is hold you close enough,
so you'll know there will always be this place of
love,
waiting for you.

My Best

I'll be honest,
today is a bad mental health day.
My battery is low, I'm struggling to engage.
I just need my bed, I'm wishing the day away.
I'm overwhelmed by household chores;
too many waking hours to be endured.
It's a day of TV and sandwiches on the floor,
then whispers of guilt saying 'you should have
done more.
Should've spent more time, put more effort in,
but I have nothing left; the rope's worn thin.
Today, the small things are insurmountable;
a shower feels just impossible.
My thoughts race, yet my body is slow.
I want the world and its demands to go.
I want to disappear, just leave me alone.
The oblivion of sleep would be absolute bliss,
and it's these luxuries I sometimes miss-
being allowed to wallow, self destruct and give
in.
But I'm a parent now, so I refuse to let it win.
That's not a choice I have left,
because my children, they deserve the best.
And my best can be different on any given day.
Some days I'm on it from the moment I wake,

a real, live Super Mum without the cape;
abuzz with energy, I'm alive and it's great.
On others, the simplest things feel hard;
so exhausting when my head is dark.
But no matter what, I'll give what I can.
My head is so noisy I struggle to plan,
but I'm trying my best; I'll give nothing less to
these people forged from my blood, my bones.
For them I'll take every bullet and stone,
bang against the glass until it caves in.
I'll fight kicking and screaming every day,
to get back to you, to us someway.
But please know that, even on my darkest days,
I'm giving the best I can, always.

My Mama Is A Princess

These early years-
they're so special.
It's easy to forget,
in the unrelenting chaos,
the chores and daily frets.
We can get lost in the slog,
the mundanity of life.
But our children, they remind us
of the reasons that we try,
that our worries matter none
because, we're their entire sky.

These moments-
they're so special.
When, amidst the toddler drama,
your daughter picks a Princess card
and all she sees is 'Mama'.
Her Mama with her tangled hair,
eyes full from broken sleep,
no fancy jewels nor ball gown;
rocking those threadbare jeans.
But to our loving little people,
we're as perfect as can be.

This life-

it is so special.
It's the beauty of Motherhood,
that on the days we feel our weakest,
we'll still be good enough.
In their eyes, a clean reflection
with no trace of previous ghosts,
just a symbol of home and safety,
when they're in our arms held close.
What an earthly privilege
to be the one whom they love most.

This time-
it is so special.
How their innocence, it shines;
their adoration too.
But only for a short time,
will we be held in such esteem.
All too soon they're teenage,
and we're straining at the seams.
So, let's savour being ethereal;
the Princess of their dreams.

I'm A Parent

I've got weetabix crusting my elbow.
Stretch marks map my thighs.
Toothpaste stains my shirt,
crumbs of sleep still in my eyes.
No time for a shower.
My hair's a knotted mess.
We're caged by towers of laundry,
but trust me, I'm trying my best.

I'm a parent.

I've forgotten to grab breakfast.
I never made the bed.
But my children have clean nappies;
they're fresh, watered and fed.
There're scatterings of mugs
filled with half-drunk tea;
I've had no time to drink them,
my lap is never free.

I'm a parent.

I'm awake amongst the stars
within these lonely, newborn nights.
Endless rounds of feeding,

of watching the sunrise.
I rock and bounce and soothe,
to curdled colic cries.
Then all at once, it's passed-
how quickly time flies!

I'm a parent.

I'm up early every morning-
most days before the sun,
to tend to little humans
that sing and squeal and run.
I wrestle arms into coats,
cajole and hurry out the door.
Buckle bodies into buggies,
and repeat forevermore!

I'm a parent.

I've mastered the art of juggling;
balancing work, laundry and play.
Sometimes it's overwhelming,
but at the end of every day,
I realise it doesn't matter
how much or little I've got done,
as long as my kids feel loved
with each rise and fall of the sun.

I'm a parent.

I'm enamoured with every inch,
every perfect piece.
In awe of what I've made
from downy crowns, to miniature feet.
I'm proud to be your parent,
with all its twists and turns.
What a privilege to see you
flourish, play and learn.

I'm a parent,
and we're our own little family.
I'm your parent;
what a precious thing to be.

I'll Carry You

I carried you in the height of summer,
my stomach engorged as swollen fruit.
Maternity smocks stretched to the seams,
struggling under the weight of two.

I carried you amidst a pandemic
unlike anything the world had ever seen.
Such devastation, uncertainty and fear
dimming the glow of pregnancy's sheen.

I carried you through the sickness;
fought nausea in crashing waves.
Took pills until I rattled;
in its grasp, I felt enslaved.

I carried you beneath my skin,
my organs shifting to make space.
My scars, a remnant of this time
now, frilled and pale like strips of lace.

I carried you for hours,
day and night against my chest.
Relentlessly pacing back and forth;
my arms, the only place you would rest.

I carried you in your first year
through every bump and stage.
Watched you change, grow and learn
to reach two years of age.

I'll carry you as an infant
and every year beyond.
No matter when or how,
if you need help I will respond.

I'll carry you forever;
you're tied within my blood.
I'll love you without conditions,
just as a parent should.

Those Early Days

The sad truth is,
the first few months of our children's lives
are rarely enjoyed as much as we'd like.
We want to savour them, freeze them in time,
keep them like precious dolls; deliciously ripe.
Whilst also, envisioning a year or two down the
line.
Like a desert mirage, we ache for and dream of
sleep;
uninterrupted, cosy and deep.
And those otherworldly, early weeks,
they pass by in an exhausted fog.
As night melts into day and we never seem to
stop,
barely get a moment to pause, soak it in;
appreciate the beauty of everything.
Because we are simply in survival mode,
adjusting to this new and heavy load.
We're bewildered with hormones running rife,
the tears streaming without knowing why.
And not only thrust into a whole new life,
but also wearing a body that no longer feels
quite right.
Our tummy, before so perfectly round,
now tender and saggy; a balloon gone down.

We're bleeding, leaking; weak and sore.
Every movement hurts, the skin angrily raw.
Yet, we need more energy than ever before.
We're expected to bounce back, push through the
pain,
whilst healing from an inner wound the size of a
dinner plate.
We're playing hostess, making constant cups of
tea,
greeting visitors in an endless stream.
We play pass the parcel with our newborns;
it's a magical time but it's also a storm.
The days are hectic but the nights can feel
lonely.
In the dark broth of night, the hours tick slowly.
There's no getting around it; sleep deprivation is
hell,
the first year akin to a spinning carousel
and sometimes, we feel we want to get off.
Just for a while, have everything stop.
It's wondrous what a bit of time can do,
a few hours of peace to reclaim the inner you.
To remember who we were before
and realise, there's no one we'd rather be more
than the Mother, the family that we are now.
That despite the battles, we'll always get through
somehow,
because those gummy smiles and cuddles tight,
and the way they fit into our arms just right,

they remind us of the magic and simple beauty
of this life.
Whether you have one baby, two or even three,
it's true; a parent is a really tough thing to be,
and there's nothing quite like those raw, early
days,
our body and heart tested in a myriad of ways.
They're fleeting as a bubble, drifting in the sky,
colours brilliant, but gone in the blink of an eye.
We wonder how our babies were ever so small,
reliving those moments as tears fall,
because those early days, they're gone in a flash,
and they're even more precious because of that.

Humans

I often look back at the end of a day,
and notice little mistakes that I've made.
I reflect; realise I could have done things a
different way.
I've argued with my toddlers, knowing that in
fact,
I should redirect, keep calm and distract;
be the rational one, use maturity and tact.
I've shouted at my babies because I couldn't
stand to hear their cries,
then felt the guilt like acid, churning me up
inside.
I've snapped, sniped and sulked, my patience
paper thin,
then hugged and kissed my children, an apology
upon their skin.
But even grown-ups reach their limit; we all
weep, break and recklessly spin.
Some days are just harder than others.
Some days, we just struggle more as Mothers.
We can only learn from past mistakes,
recognise choices we should have made,
and try to be better the next day.
We're people, not robots and it's okay for our
little ones to know,

that we have feelings too and it's healthy to let
them show.
Because they're soaking us in all the time.
They're watching and learning how to thrive;
copying us and our reactions to life.
They're looking to us to reassure and guide when
the road gets rough and emotions run high.
Of this, I try to remind myself-
the importance of managing not only mine, but
their mental health.
I want them to feel validated,
heard, respected and appreciated,
to know that whatever they feel is justified
and that, they are free to talk, to cry.
They can bring everything to me and I'll hold it
tight.
Together, there's nothing we cannot sort.
I want to know every fear and niggling thought,
so that my children know it's more than okay
to feel the hard feelings and have a bad day,
to set boundaries and accept their flaws
because, we're only humans after all.

Mummy's Poorly Brain

Today, you might wonder where Mummy's
sparkle has gone?
Who flicked the dimmer switch on the games
and fun?
I'm sure you notice when her smile isn't quite
right;
that she's doing the usual things, but her eyes
have lost their light.
But don't think for one moment, that it's
anything you've done.
For her, you're the Earth, the stars and the sun.
Just sometimes, Mummy has a poorly brain,
a head full of clouds and eyes swollen with rain.
But don't worry, soon she'll be bright once again.

Today, you may wonder why Mummy didn't get
dressed?
And why you've gone to play at Nana's, leaving
Mummy home in bed?
She still takes you to the groups, gives you
cuddles, brushes your hair
yet, somehow it seems as though she isn't truly
there.
But don't fear a single second, that it's ever
because of you.

You're the reason she continues till the daylight
bursts back through.
Just sometimes, Mummy has a poorly brain,
her thoughts colliding like a speeding train.
But don't worry, soon she'll be on track once
again.

Today, you might wonder why Mummy is quick
to yell?
Why she's all curled up, like a snail inside it's
shell?
She takes her tablets every day,
but still her mind can twist and fray.
She hopes when you're older, it'll help you to see
that we all have bad days, feel sad or angry.
And sometimes, Mummy has a poorly brain;
she fights the urge to set herself ablaze.
But don't worry, she'll show up for you always.
Anytime, any way, anyplace.

To Our Donor

I didn't pick him from a catalogue,
like shiny action men lined up on a shelf.
I didn't even see a photo,
because when I look at my children, I only want
to see myself,
not some stranger reflected back.
I would love them whatever, but truthfully, I'm
glad that they're so obviously mine;
their faces state the fact.

I chose the dark colouring so they'd feel that
they belong.
The rest comes down to nurture, teaching them
to be kind and strong.
Lea's golden locks, Daisy's swimming pool
eyes-
well, they were a beautiful, unexpected surprise.
I didn't care about his hobbies, his job nor his
build,
only that the proper health tests had been
fulfilled.

I'm still a minority but it's becoming more rife-
women longing for motherhood, with no desire
to become a wife.

Those racing against their biological clock,
looking at their lives and taking stock.
Or female partners who simply need
a little bit of help; some generous seeds.
I'm not the only one by far,
but in a room full of couples, sometimes it feels
like you are.

Battling assumptions, questions galore;
it's a part of our lives forever more.
The constant references to 'Daddy'
I'll defend my decisions everyday, gladly.
A single mum by choice, they were wanted so
badly.
I just hope that my children will understand,
and feel gratitude as I do, towards this man.
A random person somewhere in the world,
whose given me the greatest gift on earth;
a reason, a purpose, a loving family.

Motherhood in all its chaotic glory.
I'm boundlessly proud of our unique story,
and eternally thankful to the donor whose
changed me,
whose kindness transformed and utterly
reshaped me.
He's running through my daughters veins;
my twin girls, just perfect in every way.
And for them, I'm thankful

every day.

So I guess, thank you is all I can say.

Things I Want My Daughters
To Know

You are more than enough,
on your brightest and bleakest days.
You're valued, loved and appreciated
and, I'm proud of you always.

Your feelings are normal and valid.
You have a right to express, be heard.
And I'm here listening without judgement;
no fear too small nor dream absurd.

You're truly, wholly beautiful
without a shining filter.
Our imperfections make us human;
every scar, smudge and splinter.

You don't need to conform,
to change or settle just to fit in.
You're amazing as you are
so, find comfort within your skin.

Your body belongs to you;
it's your choice what to accept.
Only those you wish can touch it,
with nothing less than respect.

Your worth is not determined
by your job, income or grades.
All you need is to be happy;
find your purpose and your place.

Your life is solely yours,
to do and be all that you wish.
Ignore those who don't support you,
let them watch you bloom and flourish.

You could never let me down
or cause me to love you less.
We all make good and bad decisions
and for me, you were my best.

You are wonderful human beings-
diverse, unique and free.
You're just one person in the world
but, you're the absolute world to me.

Motherhood

Within my 2 and a half years as a Mother, I've
experienced a lot,
watched my newborns unfold into fully fledged
tots.
Once small enough to fit into the crook of each
arm,
now they crowd the room, with their energy and
charm.

I've seen little, shining teeth poke through the
gum,
like shells in the sand, bleached white by the
sun.
I've known the rapture of those first crooked
smiles,
streaked across my babies' faces, making
everything worthwhile.
The way their eyes shimmer and their arms lift;
I'm the one they want to see, and that's such a
gift.

I've heard the joyful melody as a tickle brought a
laugh,
bathed pudgy, bubbly limbs as they kicked,
grinned and splashed.

I've seen tiny, squinting faces pulled from my
womb into the light,
wrinkled and pink as chicks hatched dazedly
into life.

I've felt warm, nuzzling forms placed upon my
chest,
looked upon perfection; felt it's gentle wisps of
breath.
I've seen wobbly, tottering legs gain the
confidence to run,
and diamond droplets drench their skin, in the
paddling pool beneath the sun.

I've watched as chubby cheeks became the faces
of little girls,
as downy tufts of hair spilled into waves and
curls.
I've listened as random babbles, wails and high
pitched shrieks,
became confident sounds that morphed into
clear speech.

I remember their first bottle and first spoonfuls
of mush;
the teeny circle of their mouths, agape wide as
they could.
I've felt exhaustion, adoration and everything in
between;

a vast spectrum of colours from disheartened
grey to peaceful marine.

I've washed a million bottles, changed too many
nappies to count;
turned my fingers into spiders climbing up the
water spout.
I've left them at nursery for the first time, hands
trembling at the gate;
felt loss and relief in equal measure, handed my
heart over on a plate.

Still, it's just the beginning with so much more
to behold,
each moment a cherished photograph, gilt edged
in shining gold.
I've captured a zillion moments so I can't ever
forget,
and I can't wait to soak in and celebrate all that
will happen next.
For motherhood is an adventure, so beautifully
complex.

www.ingramcontent.com/pod-product-compliance
Lightning Source LLC
LaVergne TN
LVHW021255200726
843509LV00012B/1673